What Shapes the Land?

Bobbie Kalman

Crabtree Publishing
crabtreebooks.com

Created by Bobbie Kalman

For Barry and Liz Brissenden,
I'm so fortunate to have such great cousins (and their partners)
I love you both a lot!

Crabtree Publishing

crabtreebooks.com 800-387-7650

In Canada: We acknowledge the financial support of the Government of Canada through the Canada Book Fund for our publishing activities.

Author and Editor-in-Chief: Bobbie Kalman
Research: Robin Johnson
Editor: Kathy Middleton
Proofreader: Crystal Sikkens
Photo research: Bobbie Kalman
Design: Margaret Amy Salter, Samantha Crabtree (cover)
Production manager: Candice Campbell
Prepress technician: Katherine Kantor
Consultant: Joel Mercer, former Head of the Geography Department, Galt Collegiate Institute

Published in Canada
Crabtree Publishing
616 Welland Avenue
St. Catharines, Ontario
L2M 5V6

Published in the United States
Crabtree Publishing
347 Fifth Avenue
Suite 1402-145
New York, NY 10016

Hardcover 978-0-7787-3209-9
Paperback 978-0-7787-3219-8
Ebook (pdf) 978-0-7787-9029-7

Printed in Canada/022025/CP20250227

Illustrations:
Robert MacGregor: page 4
Margaret Amy Salter: pages 7, 11

Photographs:
© iStockphoto.com: pages 16 (inset), 29
© Shutterstock.com: front and back cover, title page, pages 3, 5, 6, 7, 8, 9, 10 (right), 11, 12, 13, 14, 15, 16 (background), 17, 18, 19, 20 (bottom), 21, 22, 23, 24, 25 (top left and bottom), 26, 27, 28, 30, 31
Other images by Corbis, Corel, and Photodisc

Library and Archives Canada Cataloguing in Publication

Kalman, Bobbie, 1947-
What shapes the land? / Bobbie Kalman.

(Looking at earth)
Includes index.
ISBN 978-0-7787-3219-8 (pbk).--
ISBN 978-0-7787-3209-9 (bound)

1. Physical geography--Juvenile literature. 2. Landforms--Juvenile literature. I. Title. II. Series: Kalman, Bobbie, 1947- . Looking at earth.

GB58.K343 2008 j551.41 C2008-905831-3

Library of Congress Cataloging-in-Publication Data

Kalman, Bobbie.
What shapes the land? / Bobbie Kalman.
p. cm. -- (Looking at earth)
Includes index.
ISBN-13: 978-0-7787-3219-8 (pbk. : alk. paper)
ISBN-10: 0-7787-3219-3 (pbk. : alk. paper)
ISBN-13: 978-0-7787-3209-9 (reinforced library binding : alk. paper)
ISBN-10: 0-7787-3209-6 (reinforced library binding : alk. paper)
1. ysical geography--Juvenile literature. 2. Landforms--Juvenile literature. I. Title. II. Series.

GB58.K35 2009
551.41--dc22
2008038132

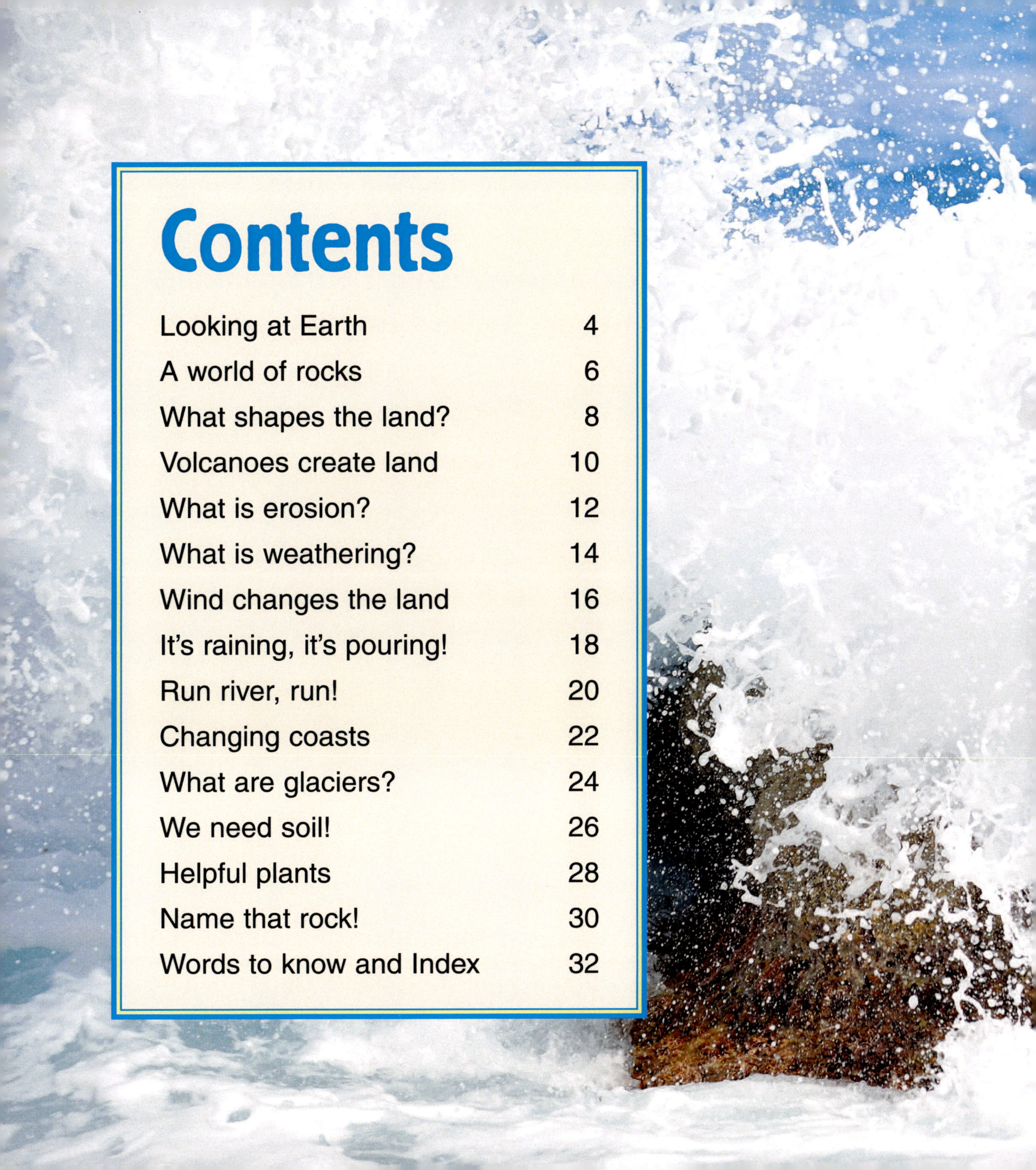

Contents

Looking at Earth

This picture shows the inside of Earth. The **crust** is the top layer of Earth. It is made of rock. We live on Earth's crust. Under the crust, there is a layer of Earth called the **mantle**. The mantle contains **magma**. Magma is red-hot melted rock.

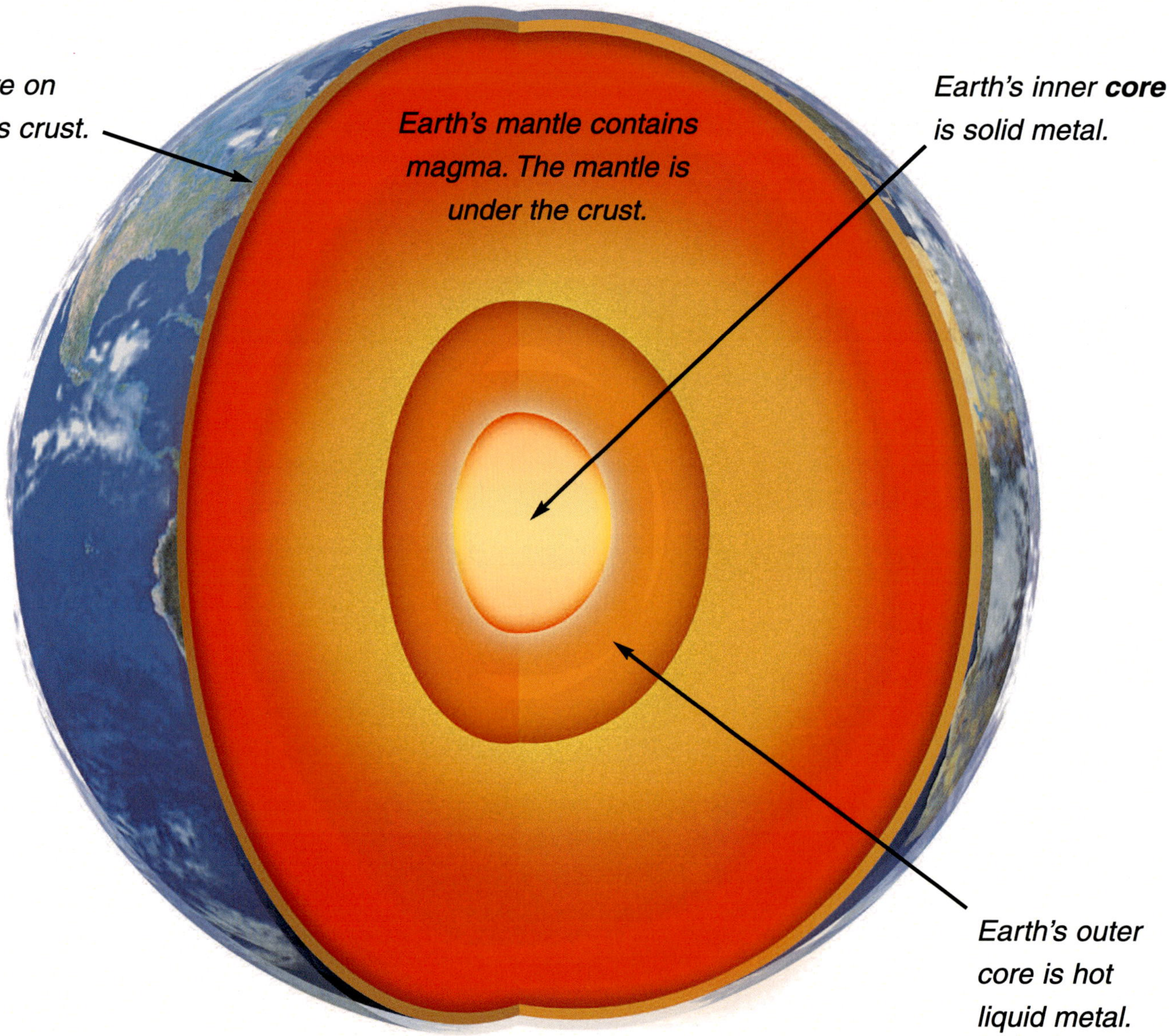

Covered up

Much of Earth's crust is covered by plants, water, and buildings. You can see Earth's crust on rocky **mountains** such as these, however.

A world of rocks

Under the plants and water on Earth, there are rocks. Rocks are made of **minerals**. There are thousands of minerals on Earth. Only a few minerals make up most rocks, however. Different minerals give rocks different colors, shapes, sizes, and **textures**. Texture is how something looks and feels. Name all the colors you see in this rock wall. Which parts might feel smooth, sharp, or rough?

Rocks of all kinds

Some rocks, such as granite, are very hard. Other rocks, such as limestone, are softer. Rocks do not stay the same. They are always changing. As they change, the shape of the land changes, too.

These large rocks are made of granite.

*The Loch Ard Gorge **cliffs** in Australia are made of soft limestone rock.*

What shapes the land?

Volcanoes destroy land and create new land. *Turn to pages 10-11 to learn how.*

Earth's crust is constantly being created and taken apart. **Landforms**, or land shapes, are made or changed by **volcanoes**, **glaciers**, wind, water, weather, and **force**. Force is strong action or movement. Most of the changes take place over a long time, but some happen quickly.

Glaciers are slow-moving bodies of ice. *Learn about glaciers on pages 24-25.*

Wind causes waves to crash onto land. Over many years, they wear down rocks. See pages 22-23 to learn how wind and waves change rocks.

*As **rivers** move, they can carve through mountains to create **valleys**. Learn about rivers on pages 20-21.*

*Strong winds blow in **deserts**. Winds carry sand from one place to another, creating **dunes**. Learn about wind and sand on pages 16-17.*

Volcanoes create land

Lava is spurting out of this volcano.

Volcanoes change the land both quickly and slowly. Volcanoes are openings in Earth's crust. They can **erupt**, or explode. When volcanoes erupt, hot liquid magma bursts out of them with great force. Magma that bursts out of volcanoes is called **lava**. Lava can destroy land, but it also creates new land.

Lava can destroy everything in its way. It can burn down forests, roads, and homes.

This picture shows lava from an underwater volcano. It is creating new land.

Mountains and islands

Lava flows down the sides of volcanoes. It cools and hardens. Hardened lava is called **basalt**, or lava rock. When volcanoes erupt many times, layers of basalt build up and create mountains. Volcanic mountains can form on land or in oceans. When volcanoes erupt in oceans, the tops of the underwater mountains become **islands**.

*This island is the top of a volcano that formed in the ocean. The volcano is **active** and still erupts. The basalt on the beach is part of new land.*

*This volcano is now a mountain on an island in Hawaii. The island is also part of the volcano. The volcano is **extinct**. Scientists believe that an extinct volcano will not erupt again, but no one can really be sure about that!*

What is erosion?

New land is created, but land is also worn down and carried away. The wearing away and moving of land is called **erosion**. Erosion changes the **landscapes** on Earth. Landscapes are all the parts of Earth that you can see, such as mountains. Wind, rain, rivers, ocean waves, and ice all **erode**, or wear away, the land on mountains, **coasts**, deserts, and other landscapes.

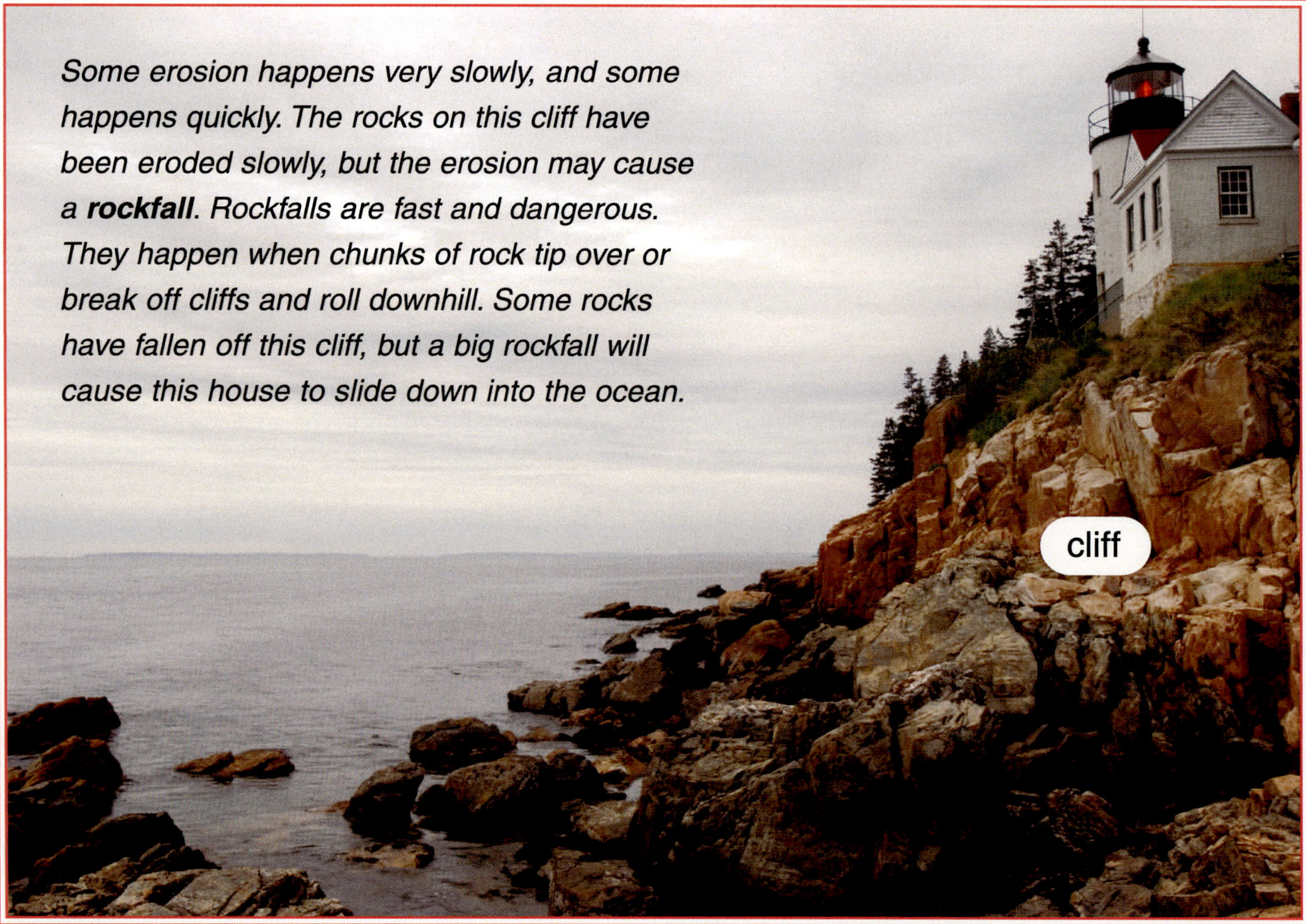

*Some erosion happens very slowly, and some happens quickly. The rocks on this cliff have been eroded slowly, but the erosion may cause a **rockfall**. Rockfalls are fast and dangerous. They happen when chunks of rock tip over or break off cliffs and roll downhill. Some rocks have fallen off this cliff, but a big rockfall will cause this house to slide down into the ocean.*

From mountains to hills

Wind blows and water carries **sediments** from place to place. Sediments are pieces of rock, sand, and soil. Sediments can wear big mountains down to rolling **hills**. Mountains are high areas of land with steep sides. Hills are small mountains with gently sloping sides.

What is weathering?

Rocks are made weak by weather. Wind, rain, snow, ice, heat, cold, and frost can all weaken rocks. This weakening is called **weathering**. One way that weather weakens and breaks up rocks is by heating and cooling them. In some places, the weather is hot during the day and cool at night. During the day, heat makes rocks **expand**, or become larger. At night, the cool air makes rocks **contract**, or become smaller. Growing and shrinking makes the cracks in rocks wider. Eventually, the rocks break into pieces.

This mountain has many cracks. Snow and ice get into the cracks and make them wider.

These rocks are full of cracks. As the cracks get bigger, pieces of the rock fall down and break apart. Rain and wind break them down into even smaller rocks. After many years, the rocks will become sediments that will be blown away by the wind.

Wind changes the land

Wind erosion lifts sand, dust, soil, and other sediments and carries them away. Wind erosion is greatest in places that have few plants, such as beaches and deserts. Without plants, there is nothing to cover the land or hold it in place. On beaches and deserts, the wind creates dunes. Dunes are moving hills of sand. Dunes change shape as the wind blows.

Blown away

In rocky areas, the wind blows sand and dirt against the rocks. Eventually, the rocks are smoothed and eroded. The wind carves new shapes in the landscape. It creates unusual **rock formations**, such as the giant mushroom on the right.

In Bryce Canyon, Utah, wind erosion has created tall, thin towers of rock called ***hoodoos****. The hoodoos have jagged edges because the wind eroded the softer layers of rock before it eroded the harder layers.*

It's raining, it's pouring!

While this girl plays in the rain, erosion is carrying away some of the soil under her feet.

When raindrops fall onto land, they loosen soil and other sediments. The sediments are then splashed away as it keeps raining. This type of erosion is called **splash erosion**. Splash erosion leaves small holes in the surface of the land. During storms or heavy rainfalls, splash erosion can cause a lot of damage to soil. The ground cannot soak up all the raindrops that fall.

When there is too much rain, the ground becomes flooded with water.

Running off with the soil

In some places, the ground is too steep or too rocky to soak up any water. In other places, the ground may be able to soak up some of the water from a rainfall, but not all. Rainwater that the ground cannot soak up is called **runoff**. Runoff trickles or flows downhill into streams, rivers, lakes, and oceans. Runoff **saturates**, or fills the land with water. It removes the thin top layer of soil and carries it away.

This land is saturated with rainwater.

Snow is melting in the mountains and flowing down the land. The runoff is taking soil with it.

Run river, run!

Some runoff flows into rivers. Rivers are fast-moving bodies of water that flow down from hills and mountains. They carry sand, stones, soil, and other sediments. Some rivers have powerful **currents**. Currents are waters flowing in a certain direction. Fast-flowing rivers can even carry **boulders**, or huge rocks. As the rivers flow, the rocks and stones bump along their bottom and sides and break off pieces of land.

This fast-flowing river made an island when it carried away the land around it.

Waterfalls and rapids

As rivers flow downhill, they erode soft rocks, leaving harder rocks behind. The hard rocks are like steps, forming waterfalls and **rapids** in the rivers. Rapids are rough, fast-flowing areas of rivers. Rivers also carve V-shaped valleys into the land. Valleys are low areas of land between hills or mountains.

These grizzly bears are fishing for salmon in the rapids and waterfalls of a fast-flowing river.

Changing coasts

A coast is the edge of land beside an ocean. Some coasts have tall, steep rocks called cliffs. Powerful winds blow ocean waves against the cliffs. The waves carry rocks and **pebbles** that cause cracks to form in the cliffs. Ocean water enters the cracks. Over time, the cracks get bigger, causing chunks of rock to fall into the ocean. These pictures show erosion on coasts.

*Ocean waves create cracks in cliffs. The cracks get bigger, and **caves** can form. Caves are holes in the sides of cliffs. A cave beside an ocean is called a **sea cave**.*

*Ocean waves break through some cliffs and create **arches** and **bridges**. A bridge is above an arch.*

*After many years, the arches break apart and the bridges fall, leaving behind **sea stacks**. All these sea stacks were part of cliffs, caves, and bridges.*

Sea stacks erode and break into smaller rocks.

Rocks become pebbles. Pebbles turn to sand.

What are glaciers?

Ice erosion is caused by glaciers. Glaciers are huge rivers of ice that form high on mountains. They form from layers of snow that pile up over many years and turn to thick blue ice. Eventually, the glaciers become so heavy that they start moving slowly downhill.

This glacier is slowly moving down from these mountains.

Changing glaciers

Glaciers form on cold mountaintops around the world. In cold countries, glaciers continue to move slowly downhill until they reach oceans. Then they break off in huge chunks called **icebergs**, and they float away.

This glacier has reached the ocean. You can see the dirt it carries.

Icebergs are large floating pieces of ice that have broken off glaciers.

Making valleys

As glaciers move, rocks and dirt stick to the front, sides, and bottom of the ice. The ice and rocks scrape down the mountains. They rub away solid rock and carve U-shaped valleys in the land. Glaciers erode mountains, but they also create new landforms, such as beautiful valleys like the one on the right.

This valley was created by a glacier.

We need soil!

All living things need soil to survive. Without soil, people could not grow food to eat. Plants and animals would die. Erosion creates soil by breaking rocks into tiny pieces, but it can also move soil from places where it is needed. **Soil erosion** is the unwanted movement of soil. Wind and water remove **topsoil** from the land. Topsoil is the thin, top layer of soil, which contains important **nutrients** that plants need in order to grow.

People cause soil erosion

People also cause soil erosion by removing trees and other plants from the land. Plants help prevent erosion. They cover and protect rocks and soil from wind and water. Plant roots help hold soil in place so it does not erode and crumble away.

Destroying plants

People clear land to build houses, farms, and roads. They also allow farm animals such as sheep and cows to **overgraze** in fields. To overgraze is to eat too many plants and grasses in one area. Without plants, rocks and soil erode quickly.

Slowing down erosion

Farmers can help stop erosion by not overgrazing their fields. They can also plant rows of trees, bushes, and other plants to protect their fields from the wind.

Too many animals grazing in an area can remove all the plants and turn soil into sand and dust.

Rows of trees stop the wind from carrying away topsoil in fields.

Helpful plants

Nature helps control erosion. Although all plants help slow erosion, **mangroves** are especially helpful at slowing erosion on coasts. Mangroves are trees that grow along or near tropical oceans. They can survive in places where most other trees would not survive. Mangroves have thick, twisted roots that help keep mud and sediments from being carried out to oceans. The mud and sediments build up to form new land. Mangroves also protect coasts from powerful ocean waves and storms.

The roots of mangroves hold soil in place and help build new land.

You can help, too!

You can help slow erosion where you live. The best way to slow erosion is to take care of the plants that protect rocks and soil. You can plant new trees, flowers, and other plants in your yard or garden, as well.

Name that rock!

Rocks are shaped by wind, water, blowing sand or soil, and ice. Rocks with unusual shapes are called rock formations. The rock formations shown here look like animals or plants. Which rock resembles an elephant, a dragon, a tree, **goblins**, or a frog? Find the answers on the next page.

This rock formation is on a beach. Which animal does it resemble?

How do you think this rock got its shape? What imaginary animal does it look like?

This rock formation is in a desert. After which animal is it named?

This rock formation is named after a large plant. Guess the name of the plant.

What kind of creatures are these?

Answers:

1. frog rock; 2. dragon; 3. elephant rock; 4. tree; 5. goblins.

Words to know

Note: Some boldfaced words are defined where they appear in the book.

arch A curved structure with an opening, which supports a bridge above it

bridge A structure that connects two parts

cliff A tall, steep wall of rock at the edge of an ocean or sea

coast A part of land beside an ocean

desert A dry area of land that is usually covered with sand and which does not have many plants growing on it

dune Sand blown by the wind into mounds

goblin An imaginary creature that looks like a short person

island Land that has water all around it

magma Hot melted rock under Earth's crust

mantle The layer under Earth's crust, which contains magma

mineral A solid substance found in rocks

mountain A high area of land with steep sides

nutrient A substance that helps things grow

pebble A small stone made smooth by water or sand

valley A low area of land between mountains or hills

volcano An opening in Earth's crust from which lava and gases shoot out; the mountain made by hardened lava

Index